Marsupials

Opossums

by Natalie Deniston

Bullfrog Books

Ideas for Parents and Teachers

Bullfrog Books let children practice reading informational text at the earliest reading levels. Repetition, familiar words, and photo labels support early readers.

Before Reading
- Discuss the cover photo. What does it tell them?
- Look at the picture glossary together. Read and discuss the words.

Read the Book
- "Walk" through the book and look at the photos. Let the child ask questions. Point out the photo labels.
- Read the book to the child, or have them read independently.

After Reading
- Prompt the child to think more. Ask: Opossums are marsupials. Moms have pouches. Can you name any other marsupials?

Bullfrog Books are published by Jump!
5357 Penn Avenue South
Minneapolis, MN 55419
www.jumplibrary.com

Copyright © 2025 Jump! International copyright reserved in all countries. No part of this book may be reproduced in any form without written permission from the publisher.

Library of Congress Cataloging-in-Publication Data

Names: Deniston, Natalie, author.
Title: Opossums / by Natalie Deniston.
Description: Minneapolis, MN: Jump!, Inc., [2025]
Series: Marsupials | Includes index.
Audience: Ages 5–8
Identifiers: LCCN 2024020174 (print)
LCCN 2024020175 (ebook)
ISBN 9798892135221 (hardcover)
ISBN 9798892135238 (paperback)
ISBN 9798892135245 (ebook)
Subjects: LCSH: Opossums—Juvenile literature.
Classification: LCC QL737.M34 D46 2025 (print)
LCC QL737.M34 (ebook)
DDC 599.2/76—dc23/eng/20240506
LC record available at https://lccn.loc.gov/2024020174
LC ebook record available at https://lccn.loc.gov/2024020175

Editor: Katie Chanez
Designer: Emma Almgren-Bersie

Photo Credits: irin717/iStock, cover; JulesA/Shutterstock, 1; IrinaK/Shutterstock, 3, 22; Cavan-Images/Shutterstock, 4; Lorna Ziegler/Shutterstock, 5; Imagebroker/Alamy, 6–7, 23tr; Karel Bock/iStock, 8; Brian Lasenby/Shutterstock, 9, 23tl; Joe McDonald/Getty, 10–11, 23br; Evelyn D. Harrison/Shutterstock, 12–13, 23bl; Jason Ondreicka/Alamy, 14; JasonOndreicka/iStock, 15, 24; Gay Bumgarner/Alamy, 16–17; Michal Ninger/Shutterstock, 18; Collins Unlimited/Shutterstock, 18–19; Daniel Borzynski/Alamy, 20–21.

Printed in the United States of America at Corporate Graphics in North Mankato, Minnesota.

Table of Contents

Hanging Out	4
Parts of an Opossum	22
Picture Glossary	23
Index	24
To Learn More	24

Hanging Out

Look in the tree.

It is an opossum!

Its den is in the tree.

It climbs.

claw

Claws help.

Mom has a pouch.

What is inside?

Joeys!

They were just born.

They are the size of honeybees.

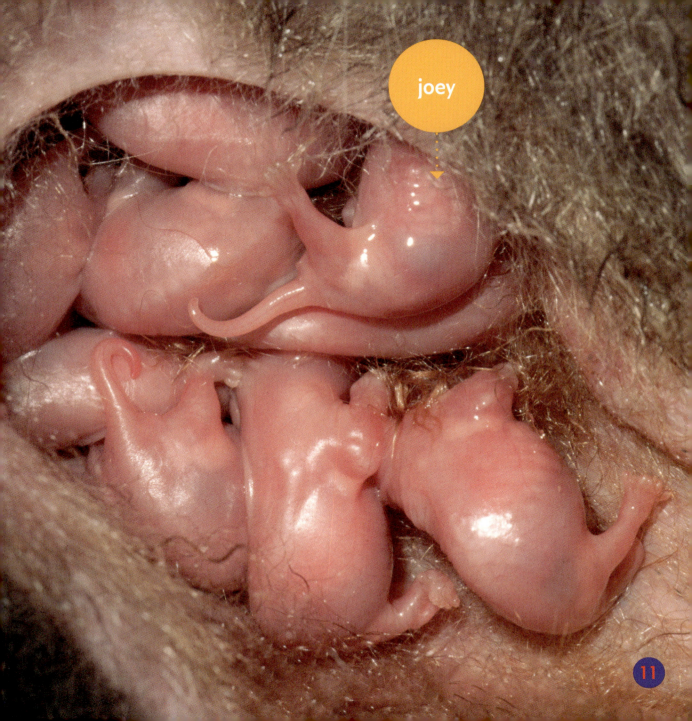joey

The joeys grow. They are too big for the pouch. They ride on Mom's back.

They climb on their own.

They hang!
How?
With their tails!

15

They look for food.

Like what?

Bugs, eggs, and plants.

They grow up.
One plays dead.
Why?
The fox will not eat it!

fox

It finds its own den.
Bye, opossum!

Parts of an Opossum

What are the parts of an opossum? Take a look!

Picture Glossary

claws
Hard, sharp nails on the feet of an animal.

den
The home of a wild animal.

joeys
Baby opossums.

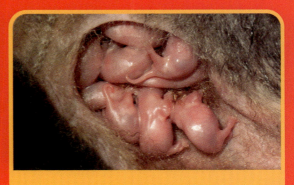

pouch
A pocket in a marsupial mother's body in which it carries its young.

Index

claws 9
climbs 8, 14
den 7, 21
food 17
grow 13, 18
hang 15
joeys 10, 13
plays dead 18
pouch 10, 13
ride 13
tails 15
tree 4, 7

To Learn More

Finding more information is as easy as 1, 2, 3.

❶ Go to www.factsurfer.com

❷ Enter "opossums" into the search box.

❸ Choose your book to see a list of websites.